Above: *The entrance block to the Royal Observer Corps No. 20 Group protected headquarters; beneath this exposed structure of steel and reinforced concrete are its hidden operations rooms and living quarters*

INTRODUCTION

The Royal Observer Corps (ROC) was founded in 1925 as the Observer Corps, after German air raids during the First World War exposed the lack of an integrated system of air defence. It was granted royal status in 1941. After the Second World War, and the advent of the Cold War, fear of nuclear war led to an arms race between the former Allies.

Britain's first atomic fission bomb, 'Blue Danube', entered service in 1953. That same year the Soviets detonated their first hydrogen, or thermonuclear (fusion) bomb, and the Home Office extended their studies on the effects of nuclear bombs.

In 1954 the ROC adopted the nuclear reporting role to gather data on any nuclear explosions and issue the appropriate warnings. The following year it was integrated with the Air Raid Warning Organisation to form the United Kingdom Warning and Monitoring Organisation (UKWMO). At the same time the Ministry of Works began

to build a series of nuclear resistant bunkers in case of war.

By the time the York bunker was built as headquarters to the ROC's No. 20 Group, in 1961, public fear of nuclear war was at its height, exacerbated by uncertainty over Soviet intentions in Berlin, and later during the Cuban Missile Crisis of 1962 and by television dramas such as 'The War Game' (1965).

The bunker is a rectangular three-storey structure built into a slope using the 'cut and cover' technique (a pit is dug, the structure built and then covered over). The underground parts were waterproofed ('tanked' in three layers of asphalt protected by brickwork). Once complete it was covered with earth at least 3ft (91.5cm) deep to increase protection against blast and heat, and to lessen the effects of penetrating radiation.

Left: *Family fall-out shelter depicted in a civil defence handbook of 1963. Such Government-issued material heightened public anxiety over nuclear war*

Above: The bunker's main corridor, at mid-level, sunk over four metres below ground

ENTRANCE BLOCK

The only exposed parts of the bunker are the entrance block (originally painted white) and the emergency escape hatch, which were built to resist the effects of blast. The walls and roof are of thick reinforced concrete, and all large openings are protected by external steel baffle plates (plates to deflect blast). The blast door to the entrance block is approached by concrete steps which gave the block its nickname, the 'Aztec temple'. It permits access to a passageway divided into an airlock by two rubber-sealed gas-proof doors to prevent the ingress of radioactive particles during nuclear attack.

The escape hatch is at the opposite end of the entrance block and is fitted with a counter-weighted hinged steel manhole cover designed to resist a pressure wave of 30 tons (30.481 tonnes). A sheltered stairway in addition to the hatch was later added (now used as the disabled access).

MID-LEVEL
Canteen

The canteen is reached from the main corridor at the mid-level of the bunker by a small passageway. The second largest room in the bunker, it was multi-functional, used for training and eating meals, and was the only room available to the staff for relaxation.

Plug-in telephone terminal boxes used for training are situated on a bar around the walls. Tables and chairs would have been stacked to the sides of the room and brought out as necessary. Today the room contains a short film giving a brief introduction to the Cold War.

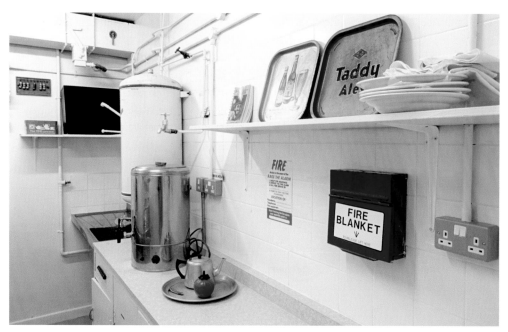

Above: Kitted out with basic 1960s equipment, the kitchen had limited space for supplies. The ROC produced its own recipe book to encourage staff to be inventive with restricted ingredients

Above: The plant room, which contains the life-support systems of the bunker, including a mixing chamber, an air-cooling system, a circulation fan, a generator and duplicated cooling pumps

Kitchen

The kitchen is off the same passageway as the canteen and is linked to it by a glazed serving hatch. It was equipped with a large catering oven, hot plate, electric cooker and toaster, and water-heaters. Storage included a tall crockery cupboard behind the door and five fitted cupboards beneath a Formica work surface. Three cupboards were allocated to the crews for their own supplies.

Plant Room

Next to the kitchen and canteen is the plant room. The room is largely taken up with air-conditioning equipment, which could be operated in four modes: 'normal' (fresh air mixed, cooled and circulated), 'modified normal' (air-cooling system turned off to save water), 'recirculation' (internal air reused), and 'filtration' (air drawn in through 'particulate filters' to remove dust or radioactive particles).

It was essential to be able to cool air drawn into the bunker, as in a nuclear situation external air temperatures could be high. In a chamber at the rear of the plant room is a stand-by diesel generator, which would start automatically if mains power was lost. Fuel for continuous running over 40 days was stored in an external underground tank, but use of the generator for any length of time would have affected air quality in the bunker.

If fall-out (radioactive debris caused by the bomb explosion) was anticipated, the bunker functioned in a similar manner to a submarine: it was 'closed up' and the air inside recirculated for as long as possible before a gulp of fresh air was drawn in through the particulate filters in 'filtration' mode, foul air expelled, and recirculation started again.

Ejector Room

As the bunker is below ground level, the wastewater system is lower than the sewage mains, necessitating the use of pressurized ejection. Sewage and wastewater were led into one of a pair of vessels, each with a float that, when the vessel was full, tripped a blast of compressed air from a cylinder to expel its contents. The cylinder was replenished by one of a pair of automatic air compressors. The equipment in both the plant and ejector rooms was duplicated in case of failures.

Above: Plotting fall-out in mirror writing on the reverse of display A in the operations room

Operations Room

At the heart of the bunker over both the mid- and lower levels is the operations room, with its associated radio, teleprinter, and telephone exchange rooms. Here the information received from the observation posts was plotted and displayed, so that damage and fall-out levels could be assessed and warning given to the civil authorities, military and public.

At the centre of the lower level (the well) of the operations room is the command table at which the senior warning officers sat. The plotters, who received information from the outlying monitoring posts, sat in the gallery in a row behind a desk fitted with rotating Perspex display boards on which they wrote the information with chinagraph pencils (designed for use on china or glass). In the opposite gallery and the well below sat the tellers (the number of whom varied), who sent out information. Six plotters were nominated as 'post-display plotters' and each would have been in telephone contact with two clusters of monitoring posts. A plotter receiving report of a nuclear explosion would shout the codeword 'Tocsin' to alert all in the operations room.

Incoming data was written on the post-display boards. At five-minute intervals the boards would be rotated, displaying the information to the operations room, while being updated on the reverse. For any single explosion data from at least three posts would have been plotted on the triangulation table to locate the ground zero (ground immediately under an exploding bomb), the power of the explosion, and whether the bomb was an air-burst or a ground-burst detonation.

This information was then transferred onto display boards in the well: display A (current situation map), B (cumulative situation

Above: The well of the operations room, below the gallery level

map), E (European situation map), and T (United Kingdom situation map).

Once fall-out was reported, the data would have been displayed on the first fall-out boards, before being transferred to the dose log charts (graphs sheets on which radioactivity levels were plotted over time), and displays A and B.

There would have been a constant exchange of the accumulating data between the tellers and the Midland Sector Control at Fiskerton near Lincoln, the adjacent group headquarters, and the various other recipients known as 'customers'.

The ROC communication equipment – teleprinters, transmitting heads and tape reperforators for gathering and transferring data – was in a sound-proofed room beneath the gallery. The communication network was designed to allow for degradation due to enemy action, enabling the communications officer to re-route information via other headquarters to maintain contact. During the operational life of the bunker, the equipment was updated on a number of occasions. By the time the bunker closed in 1991 keyboards with visual display units and the SX2000 automated message switching system had substantially simplified and sped up the process.

It became clear by the late 1960s that an attack upon Britain could be launched with the minimum of warning, and so a remote sensing device – the Atomic Weapons Detection Recognition and Estimation of Yield (AWDREY) device – was installed at 12 ROC headquarters, including York. The sensor was mounted on the roof, and the display unit was on the gallery in the operations room. Had an attack occurred AWDREY would automatically have transmitted data about the explosion to all other group and sector headquarters.

Officers' Room

The officers' room, opposite the operations room, was used by the commandant and his deputy. There were only ever three to five full-time staff employed by the Home Office at each of the ROC group headquarters; during the closing stages at York there were

'In a sense Jim and I were lucky, for although our office was cramped, we did have our own room and privacy. The crews weren't so lucky though – other than in the toilet cubicles there was no escape from one another.'

Above: Deputy Commandant David France joined the ROC in 1978 and served at York from 1986 until retirement

three: the deputy commandant, an observer, and a secretary. The commandant at York, a volunteer civilian, was responsible for the operational running of the bunker and the group, whereas the deputy commandant was responsible for the equipping, and practical running of the group.

The fittings in the room were basic: a wooden bench, a radio shelf, a coat rack, and a small wall safe. The charts on the wall and on portable boards were used to administer the running of the headquarters and the various monitoring posts dotted around the group area.

Above: Post-display plotters at York in the 1960s transferring incoming data from the monitoring posts

Dormitories

The bunker was manned by 50 to 60 ROC volunteers, British Telecommunications engineers, and Home Office scientists. The volunteers were split into three crews and were expected to operate in a 'nuclear environment' for at least two weeks. Two dormitories provided accommodation. The larger, lined by six two-tier bunks, was usually occupied by female staff, while the smaller, for men, had provision for four, giving a total of 20 beds. This necessitated a 'hot bed' system, where crew members took beds as they became available. Personal possessions could only be stored in suitcases and bags on the shelves above the beds.

Dimmer switches were installed to keep lighting levels low, but under 'recirculation' conditions, sleeping would have been difficult due to the poor quality and increased temperature of the air.

Toilets (Ablutions)

The women's toilet, roughly opposite the plant room, is a basic facility fitted with two toilet cubicles, a pair of sinks, a shower, and an electric water heater. Adjacent are the men's toilets (now modernized), which were similarly basic, but smaller, with only one toilet cubicle, a urinal, a sink, and a shower.

Telephone Exchange

The bunker originally had a manual telephone exchange manned by volunteer General Post Office (GPO) operators. The equipment was updated on a number of occasions, and the exchange became the British Telecommunications (BT) equipment room. The final configuration used the computer-controlled SX2000 digital private automatic branch exchange (PABX), capable of dialling its extensions directly, without the need for an exchange. Later the cypher message switching system (MSX) was introduced, allowing faster data transfer rates.

The copper cables required of a telephone system are vulnerable to blast damage and electromagnetic pulse (EMP), both effects of a nuclear explosion, so where possible cables were laid underground and the SX2000 exchange was enclosed in a shielded cabinet. Nevertheless, in case of failure of the telephone circuits, the bunker had a radio room equipped with very high

Above: The spartan women's dormitory, with an ROC uniform laid out on one of the bunks

Above: The telephone exchange, with the shielded SX2000 cabinet on the left

frequency (VHF) RN2 and RN4 'highway' radio systems. The aerial was mounted on an extendable mast near the entrance block and the equipment was protected from EMP by earthing straps attached to the walls to form a Faraday cage (an earthed metal screen).

UPPER LEVEL
Radiator Room

The radiator room houses the cooling fan and radiator of the stand-by diesel generator in the plant room below. It also contains two carbon dioxide fire-extinguishers. Air vents in the eastern and southern wall have louvred steel shutters that would have automatically closed had a blast wave occurred. The room, rendered radioactive by the blast, would have been shut off by the steel door sealed closed using four wedge handles.

Decontamination Rooms

The doorway to the left of the outer air-lock door leads into a pair of interlinked decontamination rooms. Anyone exposed to fall-out outside the bunker would have entered the first room, stripped, placed their contaminated clothing in the 'hot box' (a waist-high brick bin), and showered in the sink provided. They would then have proceeded into the next room (currently the ticket office), washed again, checked themselves and been checked for radioactive particles by a fellow member of staff using a radiacmeter, and dressed in clean clothing.

Aerosol Filter Chamber

This room contains two banks of gas, or particulate, filters that would have removed any microscopic radioactive particles in the air drawn into the structure during 'filtration' mode. The filters could not be cleaned or replaced when saturated. After a nuclear attack 'filtration' mode would have been used sparingly, as the filter banks would have become congested. The rate of congestion depended on the size of the indrawn radioactive particles. When the ROC was stood down in 1991 there were still large boxes of the service ration 'Biscuits Brown', dated 1962, stored in this room.

Above: The cooling fan in the radiator room in early 1992

Above: The dressing room, attached to the decontamination room, in early 1992 shortly after stand-down

Above: The aerosol filter chamber, with its boxes of service ration 'Biscuits Brown' dating from 1962

Above: *The Soviet Union's first nuclear test, on 29 August 1949, at Semipalatinsk in north-east Kazakhstan*

THE DAWN OF NUCLEAR THREAT

The United States changed the course of military history by detonating the world's first atomic device, 'Gadget', in the New Mexico desert on 16 July 1945, on the eve of the last conference of the Second World War between the allies, held at Potsdam, Germany. Two weeks later, on 6 August, a Boeing B-29 Superfortress bomber, *Enola Gay*, dropped

'From Stettin in the Baltic to Trieste in the Adriatic an iron curtain has descended across the Continent.'
Sir Winston Churchill, Fulton, Missouri, 5 March 1946

the first atomic bomb, 'Little Boy', on Hiroshima, devastating 5 square miles (13km²) with the force of about 15 kilotons of trinitrotoluene (TNT). A second B-29 bomber, *Bock's Car*, dropped another atomic bomb, 'Fat Man', on Nagasaki three days later, with an explosion of about 21 kilotons. The full horror of the atomic bomb had been demonstrated to the world. The Japanese Government surrendered on 16 August 1945, bringing about the end of the Second World War.

THE COLD WAR BEGINS

In his famous 'iron curtain' speech at Fulton, Missouri on 5 March 1946, Winston Churchill acknowledged the fears that the peace since the end of the Second World War would not last. The advent of the Cold War witnessed a variety of measures to restore Britain's defensive capability, including the reconstitution of the ROC on 1 January 1947.

On 29 August 1949 the relationship between the Western Allies and the Soviet Union took a dramatic turn for the worse when a Soviet nuclear device was detonated at Semipalatinsk, spurring on the 'arms race' and adding impetus to Britain's fledgling nuclear weapons programme, and the need to consider the nation's ability to survive the effects of a nuclear attack.

EMERGENCY PLANNING

The Home Office undertook a number of research projects to determine the effects of nuclear explosions, but with the first test detonation of the United States's hydrogen bomb in 1952, the true scale of the problem became evident. It was realized that under typical weather conditions, the fall-out plume produced by a 10-megaton thermonuclear bomb dropped over Birmingham would reach the Norfolk coast in nine hours.

The major effects produced by a nuclear explosion would be flash (light), blast (shockwave and sound), thermal radiation (heat), initial radiation (released by the explosion), residual radiation (fall-out) and electromagnetic pulse (EMP).

The first four effects would devastate the immediate vicinity of the ground zero, while the insidious fifth effect would have the potential to cause thousands of additional casualties in areas many tens or even hundreds of miles away. The final effect, EMP, would not affect human health, but would cause massive induction surges in unprotected electrical circuits, particularly those using transistors, and so potentially destroy all manner of electrical and communications equipment.

The lethal effects of fall-out could be minimized if there was sufficient warning of its approach, and radioactivity levels were monitored. In 1954 the role of nuclear monitoring and reporting was allocated to the ROC, a volunteer civilian organization whose members were drawn from all walks of life. It was administered by the Air Ministry and originally associated with the RAF, with a similar uniform, which it kept to aid recruitment.

It operated as a component of the United Kingdom War Monitoring Organisation (UKWMO), responsible for public warning of air attack (conventional or nuclear), confirmation of a nuclear attack, public warning of the approach of fall-out, supplying Government headquarters, home defence

forces, and neighbouring countries with details of nuclear bursts and a scientific assessment of the path and intensity of fall-out, and providing a post-attack meteorological service.

The ROC was loaned by the War Office to the Home Office, which also had under its authority the civil defence organization, with responsibility in case of nuclear attack, together with the emergency services and the local authorities, for the assistance of the public.

The country was divided up into Civil Defence Regions, Sub-Regions, and Districts. All levels of Government departments, local authorities, councils, police, and health and emergency services had a role to play. Under nuclear attack this system would likely become fragmented, and to counter this protected Government headquarters, utilities control and repair depots, rescue depots, and 'buffer' (food) depots were established in each Civil Defence Region to work independently of central Government for as long as was necessary.

The public was kept informed by the dissemination of advice through leaflets and public information broadcasts at cinemas and over the television and radio. It was hoped that

Above: A civil defence poster issued by the British Government in 1957, showing the effects of a nuclear bomb

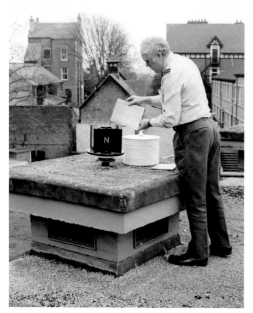

Above: A member of the ROC changes the cassette of the ground zero indicator at the York bunker

the work of the ROC and the civil defence would ensure the protection and succour of members of the population surviving a nuclear attack, whether those surviving a direct attack, or those affected indirectly by fall-out.

NUCLEAR MONITORING

The Ministry of Works began work on designs for nuclear-resistant bunkers for the ROC in 1955. They produced three designs of bunker: an underground monitoring post, a 'semi-protected' (surface) group headquarters, and a 'protected' (semi-underground) group headquarters. A prototype underground monitoring post was built in 1956 at Upper Hale, Farnham, Surrey. With minor alterations, it became the standard design for all 1,561 posts that were built across the country.

The York bunker was built on Government land behind a Victorian villa called Shelley House and was opened on 16 December 1961 by the Earl of Scarborough.

It comprised an office block, a training hut, an isotope store (for calibrating instruments), and a protected headquarters (the No. 20 Group control) bunker. It was not capable of surviving a direct hit, but was designed to resist the effects of a near hit and a radioactive environment.

The monitoring posts were grouped together in clusters of three or four to aid communications and the accurate triangulation of a nuclear burst. Each cluster had a dedicated telephone circuit linking one post to another and to the group headquarters. One of the posts was also nominated as the master post and was fitted with radio equipment in case of damage to telephone lines.

All headquarters bunkers and monitoring posts were equipped with a ground zero indicator, to obtain the bearing, elevation, and spot size of a nuclear detonation, a bomb power indicator, to measure the overpressure of a blast wave, and a fixed survey meter, to measure radiation levels. In addition some posts were equipped as meteorological stations to measure wind speeds and direction, which would determine the rate and direction of travel of any fall-out dust. These posts were known as ROCMET posts.

The volunteers who manned the bunkers attended evening and weekend training sessions, and undertook two major exercises a year. In peacetime the group headquarters was manned by a permanent staff of three, while the outlying monitoring posts were unmanned. It was only during training exercises or if war threatened that the whole system would be manned.

Above: ROC summer training camp at RAF Coningsby in Lincolnshire, 1967

Above: The RAF's V-Force in 1959; Britain's nuclear strike force comprised the Vulcan, the Valiant and the Victor aircraft

THE CUBAN MISSILE CRISIS

One of the tensest periods of the Cold War was the Cuban missile crisis of 1962. The Soviet Union established a number of SS-4 and SS-5 nuclear missile launch sites on the island of Cuba that directly threatened the United States of America. The situation became so grave that on 24 October the US armed forces went to DEFCON 2 (the highest state of preparation for war), and in Britain RAF-manned Thor intermediate-range ballistic missiles were fuelled and readied for launching, and elements of the RAF's V-Force prepared for war.

The crisis was averted by negotiation on 28 October: President Kennedy agreed that the United States would not invade Cuba in exchange for President Khrushchev's agreement to dismantle the missiles on the island. Kennedy also secretly agreed to the removal of Jupiter missiles from Turkey.

Although the UKWMO was fully prepared to call out the ROC during the crisis, the point at which the order would have been given was never reached. If war had broken out, the UKWMO would have been given advance warning of any potential air attacks by the United Kingdom Regional Air Operations Centre at High Wycombe, which received data from the North American Air Defence System, NATO, the United Kingdom Air Defence Ground Environment, and the Ballistic Missile Early Warning System at RAF Fylingdales.

OPPOSITION TO NUCLEAR THREAT

In 1956 the Government announced that Britain was going to reduce its conventional forces and instead would switch to a policy of nuclear deterrence. There was widespread opposition to the decision, which grew during the deployment of the V-Force and Thor missiles during the late 1950s.

Above: The Ballistic Missile Early Warning System at RAF Fylingdales in Yorkshire in May 1967

In 1958 the first of what became an annual march to the Atomic Weapons Research Establishment at Aldermaston was held. Opposition groups developed, including the Committee of 100, and the Campaign for Nuclear Disarmament (CND). The CND had members from all political parties but was predominantly allied to left-wing politics and was supported by influential Labour politicians including Tony Benn and Michael Foot.

The protest movement swelled during the late 1970s and early 1980s as a consequence of political, economic, and moral opposition to the replacement of the Royal Navy's Polaris missile, and the American deployment of Pershing and Cruise missiles in Europe.

Above: Canon John Collins (centre) on the annual march from Aldermaston in Berkshire to London in April 1962. He was, together with the philosopher Bertrand Russell, one of the founding members of the CND

By the 1980s direct action protests were becoming more common, with the blockading and invading of military complexes, and interference with nuclear convoys. Some of the ROC's underground monitoring posts were targeted and it issued instructions that if one were attacked while manned the codeword 'orange' should be included in a message to request police assistance.

Among the most famous of the anti-nuclear protests were the peace camps at RAF Greenham Common, RAF Molesworth, and Menwith Hill.

THE END OF THE COLD WAR

Though tensions rose and fell during the Cold War, the ROC was never called upon fully to man its nuclear monitoring system. The disintegration of the Soviet-influenced Eastern Bloc and the opening up of the Berlin Wall in 1989 led to the end of the Cold War and the eventual stand-down of the ROC on 30 September 1991.

A small cadre of ROC volunteers was retained to assist with the manning of the military Nuclear Reporting Cell at RAF Holmpton. At the York bunker one full-time ROC officer, an observer, and a civilian secretary stayed on until 31 March 1992 to oversee the closure of the posts.

The York bunker deteriorated; equipment was left to rust, fungus grew on the walls and paint peeled in the underground damp, until in 2000 English Heritage recognized its value and took it into care.

FURTHER READING

H Buckton *Forewarned is Forearmed* (Leatherhead, 1993)
N Calder *Nuclear Nightmares* (London, 1979)
C Chant and I Hogg *The Nuclear War File* (London, 1983)
W D Cocroft and R J C Thomas *Cold War: Building for Nuclear Conflict 1946–1989* (London, 2002)
A Fursenko and T Naftali *One Hell of a Gamble: The Secret History of the Cuban Crisis* (London, 1997)
J Isaacs and T Downing *Cold War* (London, 1998)

N J McCamley *Secret Cold War Nuclear Bunker* (Barnsley, 2007)
C McCutcheon (ed.) *Protect and Survive, Civil Defence Manual of Basic Training* (Chalford, 1949)
N Spence *Watchers over the Broad Acres: The Story of the R.O.C. in Yorkshire* (Harrogate, 1987)
R J C Thomas 'No. 20 Group Royal Observer Corps Protected Headquarters', *EHHR* vol. 3 (2008), 136–147
D Wood *Attack Warning Red: The Royal Observer Corps and the Defence of Britain 1925–1992* (Portsmouth, 1976)